# Soul Mates

A Gift For

From

Copyright © 2014 Hallmark Licensing, LLC

Published by Hallmark Gift Books,
a division of Hallmark Cards, Inc.,
Kansas City, MO 64141
Visit us on the Web at Hallmark.com.

All rights reserved. No part of this publication may be reproduced, transmitted, or stored in any form or by any means without the prior written permission of the publisher.

Editorial Director: Carrie Bolin
Written and Compiled by Stacey Donovan
Editor: Kim Schworm Acosta
Art Director: Chris Opheim
Designer: Mary Eakin
Production Designer: Dan Horton

ISBN: 978-1-59530-852-8
BOK2160

Printed and bound in China
JUN14

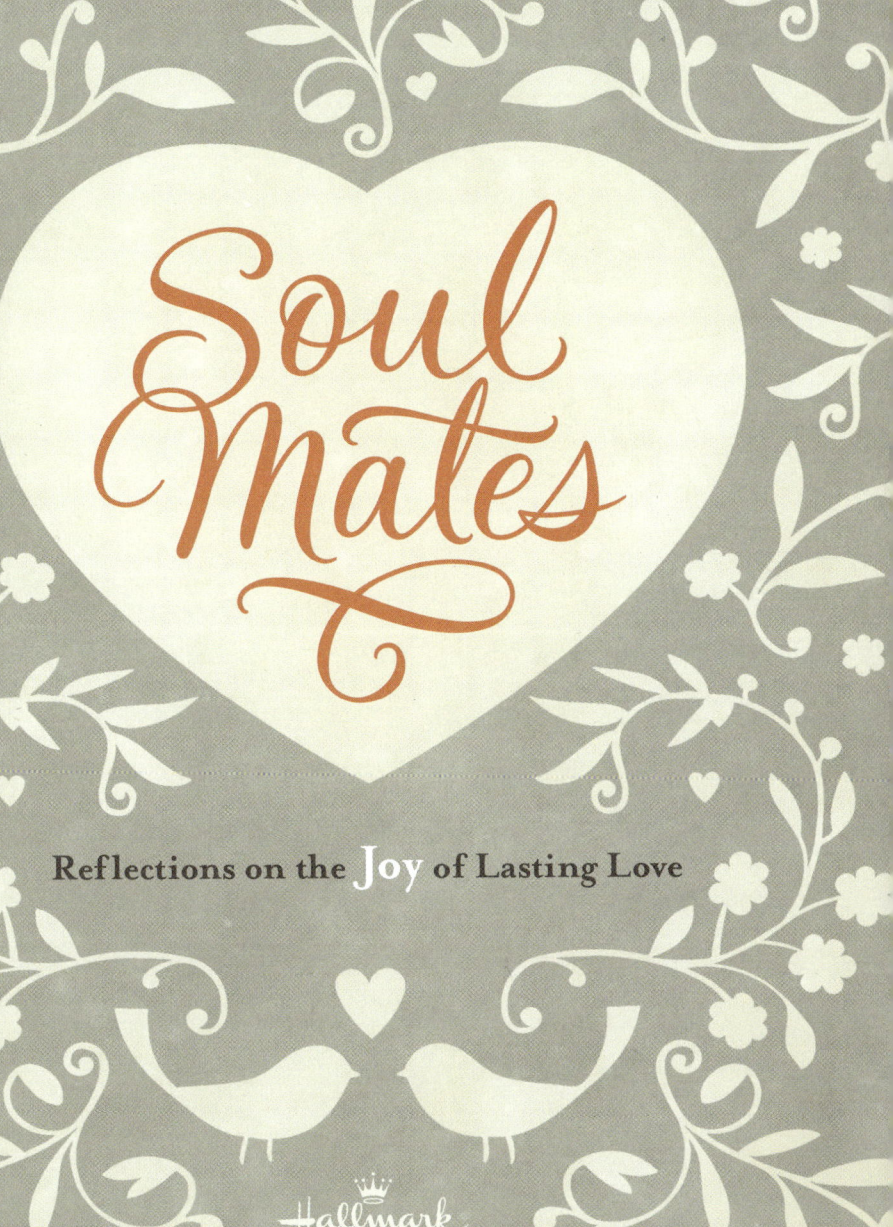

# CONTENTS

6 Discovery

30 Commitment

50 Joy

80 **Challenge**

106 **Renewal**

# Discovery

# Finding "The One"

Maybe it was a look or a smile.
Maybe it was spark between two friends
that turned into an unexpected flame.
It might have been a shared joke
that made you realize
you wanted most of your jokes to be shared.
Some people think it happens by chance,
and some are sure it was meant to be:
the way two souls
recognize each other and know,
"There you are . . .

**just the person I was looking for."**

# Come here often?

Some couples have stories of love at first sight. Others talk about a friendship that grew into something more. No matter what, something special about the other person captured their attention. We asked people what attracted them first about their partners:

"I liked his smile, his laugh, and his long, curly eyelashes. Even with an eyelash curler and many coats of mascara, I could never have lashes so lovely."

"She laughed at my jokes—even the unfunny ones—and she made me laugh, too."

"He said he'd call me, and he did. He asked me out. He opened the door for me. He paid for dinner. He called me again. I never had to wonder or overthink with him. He made it all so easy."

"How easy it was to be around her for a long time without it seeming like a long time."

"His hotness didn't hurt. But it was his kindness that did it . . . He washed dishes the first time he ate at my house (while all the other guys sat on their butts); he did my laundry because my apartment didn't have a washer. He bought me bell hooks books because he was interested in knowing me better. But more important, he was kind and gentle to everyone."

"He likes to cook. I like to eat. So, basically, I knew we were going to be a perfect match."

{ **What first attracted you to one another?** }

# A Love Story

"Boy meets Girl.
Girl wants to run
like the wind.
(She's had her share
of heartache.)
But she stays.
(She discovers Boy's
had his share
of heartache, too.)
So they both stay.
And they learn to trust.
And love."

RENEE DANIELS

"**Whatever our souls are made of,**

his and mine are the same."

EMILY BRONTË

# Questions to Get to Know Each Other Better
(for new couples and not-so-new couples)

- Vanilla or chocolate?
- Gold or silver?
- City or country?
- Creamy peanut butter or chunky?
- What's your favorite color?
- What's your favorite holiday?
- What would a perfect Saturday be like?
- What's the weirdest food you've ever eaten?
- What's a bad movie that you still kind of like?
- What's one of the silliest things you've ever done?
- What are some of your pet peeves?
- What are some of your guilty pleasures?

- What's one of your prized possessions?
- Have you ever gone skinny-dipping?
- Have you ever gotten a haircut you regretted?
- When you were little, what did you want to be when you grew up?
- If you won a million dollars, what would you do with the money?
- Do you believe in aliens?
- Do you believe in angels?
- What's something you really like about yourself?
- Were you born this amazing, or did it take some practice?

# Soul Mates in History

## Annie Oakley and Frank Butler

When Frank Butler came to Cincinnati as part of a variety show, he claimed he could beat any local marksman. He wasn't expecting a young woman, Annie Oakley, to challenge him—let alone beat him! Annie won not only the shooting contest but also his affection, and the two were married soon after. They developed an act together and toured with Buffalo Bill's Wild West show. Annie and Frank's story, immortalized in the Broadway musical *Annie Get Your Gun,* is a reminder that you never know when you might meet your costar in life.

# Pet Names

Do you have sweet, romantic, or downright goofy nicknames for each other? Lots of couples do. Here's a list of some of the usual and unusual ways people in love address each other. Are yours on the list? Do you see one you'd like to start using? (Or one that you want to tell your partner to never, ever call you?)

"How about Princess Pookie Bear?"

| | |
|---|---|
| Honey | Boo |
| Darling | Sugar |
| Handsome | Sexy |
| Papi | Lover |
| Beautiful | Mi Amor |
| Dear | Gorgeous |
| Treasure | Big Daddy |
| Love | Baby Cakes |
| Princess | My Lady |
| Bear | Cutie Pie |
| Sweetheart | Sugar Momma |
| Sweetie | Sunshine |
| Babe | Honey Bunch |
| Pumpkin | Tiger |
| Baby Girl | Pookie |
| Snookums | |

# What Kind of Soul Mates Are You?
Take our quiz and find out!

**If there's one thing you two love doing, it's . . .**
- A) wine tasting
- B) going to big parties
- C) working on your own projects
- D) spending time in the garden

**If there's one thing you two hate doing, it's . . .**
- A) shopping at a big discount store
- B) going to foreign films
- C) making small talk
- D) getting dressed up for a formal event

**A perfect weekend together might include . . .**
- A) a dinner at a fine restaurant
- B) a rock concert
- C) a visit to a bookstore
- D) a long bike ride

**You've just won your dream home in a sweepstakes! It is . . .**
- A) a luxury penthouse condo in a big city
- B) a suburban home with a heated pool, barbecue pit, and home theater
- C) a church that's been converted into a house
- D) a log cabin in the mountains

**If one of you got a tattoo (or another tattoo), it would probably be . . .**
- A) we wouldn't
- B) a cute conversation starter
- C) a meaningful quote or symbol
- D) a wild animal

**You would most enjoy working for a company that . . .**
- A) had a fancy office building
- B) sponsored fun events during work hours
- C) let you make a lot of your own decisions
- D) had good environmental practices

**If you two could own a business that was guaranteed to make you lots of money, it would be . . .**
- A) a fashion boutique
- B) a toy store
- C) an art gallery
- D) an apple orchard

**What's your favorite TV show that you watch together?**
- A) an award-winning drama
- B) a hilarious sitcom
- C) a sci-fi series
- D) you don't have a favorite show you both watch

**You would feel right at home in . . .**
- A) Paris
- B) Disneyland
- C) Portland, OR
- D) Grand Canyon National Park

**Hey, what would you like for dessert?**
- A) tiramisu
- B) a cupcake
- C) green tea ice cream
- D) apple pie

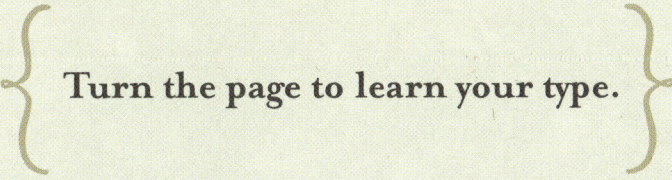

**Turn the page to learn your type.**

# What Kind of Soul Mates Are You?

## If you chose mostly A's, you are . . .

**Sophisticated Soul Mates**
You two are classy without even trying. It's no wonder you showed exceptional taste in choosing each other.

## If you chose mostly B's, you are . . .

**Fun-Loving Soul Mates**
You two are the life of the party. In fact, it wasn't even a party until you showed up. You'll never, ever get bored with each other.

## If you chose mostly C's, you are . . .

**Creative Soul Mates**
You have such a unique perspective on life, not everyone understands you . . . but you understand each other perfectly.

## If you chose mostly D's, you are . . .

### Natural Soul Mates
Both of you are in tune with the earth around you, and your love itself is a force of nature.

## If your answers are all over the board, you are . . .

### Whimsical Soul Mates
It's hard to say what either of you will do or try next, but luckily, you're both good at keeping up with each other!

like **mac and cheese**
like a wink and a smile
like needle and thread
like the sand and the shore
like cake and ice cream
like day and night
like hopes and dreams
like hugs and kisses
like my heart and yours . . .

xo

some things just go together.

oxoxox

# Commitment

# Beginning a Life Together

"When love shows up,
it doesn't leave you
where it found you.
It grabs both of you
by the hand and
takes you on the
journey of a lifetime.
Along the way,
the two of you find happiness
you never knew existed.
You see hopes and
dreams come true.
But there at the
heart of things
is the love that
started it all . . .
lighting the way . . .
helping you grow . . .
stronger and closer,
together."

SUZANNE BERRY

"Is it just me, or does this feel forever-ish?"

> "It's not just you. No 'ish' about it."

# Things Every Couple Needs . . .
## Some of these can go on a registry.
## And some can't.

- "our song" . . . even if it's not the kind of thing you slow-dance to!
- cereal bowls that are just the right size
- a kitchen gadget that makes you feel like fancy chefs
- optimism
- plenty of towels
- carry-on luggage for romantic getaways
- forgiveness

- a dark-colored quilt or comforter that won't get ruined by spilled coffee or wine
- a sense of humor
- a set of decent kitchen knives
- nice dishes that you can use all the time, not just on fancy occasions
- love

> **In vain have I struggled.**
> It will not do.

My feelings will not be repressed.

You must allow me to tell you
how ardently I admire and love you."

JANE AUSTEN, *Pride and Prejudice*

# On Your Wedding Day

- Have something to eat and drink some water. You don't want to pass out!

- Find a little time before the ceremony or during the reception for the two of you to be alone.

- Double-check you've got the rings.

- Take time to look around you and remember everyone's smiling faces . . . especially each other's.

- Don't worry about whether your guests are having fun. That's their issue.

- Know that everything will not go exactly as planned, and you wouldn't want it to. (That goes for the rest of your lives together, too.)

# Wedding Prayer

Lord, behold our family here assembled.
We thank you for this place in which we dwell,
for the love that unites us,
for the peace accorded us this day,
for the hope with which we expect the morrow,
for the health, the work, the food,
and the bright skies that make our lives delightful;
for our friends in all parts of the earth.

ROBERT LOUIS STEVENSON

# Soul Mates in History

### Queen Victoria and Prince Consort Albert

When twenty-year-old Queen Victoria proposed to her visiting cousin Albert, not everyone thought it was a good idea. For one thing, he was German. She chose the color white for a wedding dress, which some people also found unusual, but her wedding was so fabulous that white bridal gowns came into fashion and stayed there. The wedding night must have been even more fabulous, because Victoria wrote in her diary,

{ "I NEVER, NEVER spent such an evening!!! MY DEAREST DEAREST DEAR Albert . . . his excessive love & affection gave me feelings of heavenly love & happiness I never could have *hoped* to have felt before!" }

Many years later, Queen Victoria and her prince were still crazy about each other. Any couple with a love that lasts like that feels a little bit like royalty.

"Life is short, but love is good.
And love means life together.
May moonlight lay a feather
Everywhere your heads will rest.
Now yes can last forever,
Which is heaven's neighborhood.
Two souls have set the table
And Love's the honored guest.
So pour the wine and savor
Every drop of rain and trouble.
May the better and the worse
Leave only honey on your tongue.
Now words are sweet as kisses
And joy arrives redoubled.
Two hearts feast on the light
Of all the golden days to come."

JIM HOWARD

" The wedding day is
really just that . . . a day.
One big happy day of
good cake and fancy clothes.
And even though
most of the days to follow
are probably more about
laundry and leftovers,
there are still couples who
reach 'married life' and seem
just as in love as ever—
who keep a little of that
wedding-day glow—
happy simply to be living
life's big days and every days together.
And you know what?
Those are the couples
who've got it all figured out.
After all, a wedding's
a beautiful beginning . . .
but it's the 'ever after' that counts. "

SUZANNE BERRY

Joy

# Fireflies

Time flies,
but the best moments
flicker and shine.
Now here, now gone,
but there's another one
over there, and another.
All we have to do is pay attention.
So many little lights in our lives . . .

**so many reasons to be grateful.**

# Things to Compliment Your Partner On

his dependability

her optimism

her smile that lights up your mood

his butt

her craft project

his taste in music

her strong faith

his fun ideas

her cleverness at parenting

how nice he is to your mom

her genius at parallel parking

his outfit

the way she smells

how creative he is

how hard she works

his strong hands

her cute feet

his sense of humor

her loyalty

his lawn care

her hair

his knowledge

her sense of style

his kisses

her eyes

# This is a very incomplete list!
### Remember, it's OK to exaggerate . . .

## "You are literally the best dancer on the planet."

### It doesn't even count as a lie.

(Super-secret secret: Sometimes honesty is overrated.)

> **A happy marriage**
> is what happens when two people decide

to just keep dating each other,
**discovering each other,**
getting to know and love each other better
year after sweet, beautiful year."

KEELY CHACE

# A Feast for the Senses

We experience the world through sight, sound, touch, smell, and taste. Here are some ways to indulge more in the enjoyment that the five senses bring.

## Sight

- Take a drive to admire the leaves in autumn.
- Repaint a room in one of your very favorite colors.
- Take a look inside the most beautiful historic building in town.
- See a parade.

## Sound

- Go to a bagpipe performance.
- Hang a wind chime near your back door.
- Sit on a porch and listen to the crickets on a hot summer night.
- Enjoy the crackling sounds of a fire in the winter.

## Touch

- Treat yourselves to cozy flannel or sleek satin sheets.
- Get your partner to brush or comb your hair.
- Play in the snow.

## Smell

- Sample different fragrances together at a perfume counter.
- Tour a coffee-roasting facility.
- Use aromatherapy products in the bath.
- Smell the roses in a rose garden.

## Taste

- Try out a new ethnic cuisine.
- Include a vegetable you've never tried with dinner.
- Go on a quest to identify the best ice-cream flavor in the world.
- Make a loaf of homemade bread.

If you practice having fun
often enough,
you will get very good at it.

# What's on Your Shared Bucket List?

You're probably familiar with the idea of making a list of all the things you want to do in your lifetime—big, small, and in-between. What are some of the things you'd like to do together? Here are some ideas just to get you thinking:

- run a 5K . . . or a marathon
- write a book
- learn a foreign language
- learn to play a musical instrument
- own a home
- see the northern lights
- skydive
- sleep under the stars
- drop a bad habit
- visit Paris
- visit Las Vegas
- raise money for charity
- volunteer at a homeless shelter

> Once you have a list, you can think about how to make those things happen. And of course, half the fun is in the dreaming.

- jump in puddles on a rainy day
- attend a black-tie event
- get a dog
- raise a child
- make a birthday cake from scratch
- swim with dolphins
- ride an elephant
- catch a fish
- jump into a pool while wearing normal clothes
- see a movie at a drive-in
- celebrate a twenty-fifth and/or fiftieth anniversary
- live every day to its fullest

# We may not live in a dream house,

but we live in a home

where we encourage each other's dreams.

We may not travel

to every country in the world,

### but we've found the kind of love
that some search the world for and never find.

# Anniversary Gifts for Your First Through Your Sixtieth Anniversary

Here are gift themes for every year, because they *all* deserve to be celebrated, along with gift ideas. If you make it past sixty, you get to start all over again! (And of course, you don't have to wait for an anniversary to use any of these ideas.)

|    | Theme | Gift idea |
| --- | --- | --- |
| 1 | paper | a book of "love coupons" |
| 2 | cotton | plush terry bathrobe |
| 3 | leather | shoes |
| 4 | fruit/flowers | chocolate-dipped strawberries |
| 5 | wood | go out for wood-fired pizza |
| 6 | candy | spell out a romantic message in gummy candy letters |
| 7 | wool | a sweater that matches their eyes |
| 8 | pottery | a flowering plant in a decorative planter |
| 9 | willow/wicker | a new picnic basket for a picnic in the park |
| 10 | tin/aluminum | a retro lunchbox to take to work |
| 11 | steel | an ice bucket filled with their favorite beverage |
| 12 | silk | luxe pajamas |

| | | |
|---|---|---|
| 13 | lace/textile | a fresh addition to their closet |
| 14 | ivory | cruelty-free, please! go to a piano bar or piano concert |
| 15 | crystal | a single rose in a crystal vase |
| 16 | coffee/tea | a before-work breakfast date |
| 17 | wine/spirits | invent a new cocktail and name it after her |
| 18 | appliances | a waffle iron that makes heart-shaped waffles |
| 19 | jade | a dinner at a Chinese restaurant with "jade" in the name |
| 20 | china | a personalized mug or cereal bowl |
| 21 | fire | a romantic dinner at home lit by twenty-one candles |
| 22 | water | visit a local aquarium |
| 23 | air | decorate the bedroom with balloons |
| 24 | stone | visit the spa for a hot-stone massage |
| 25 | silver | silver jewelry with an engraved message |
| 26 | art | a date at the local art museum |
| 27 | music | make them a custom music mix |
| 28 | linens | high thread-count sheets . . . put them to good use ☺ |
| 29 | tools | any new "tool" for their favorite hobby or pastime |

| | | |
|---|---|---|
| 30 | pearl | anything adorned with mother-of-pearl accents |
| 31 | travel/tourism | be "tourists" in your own state and see something new |
| 32 | bronze | a classy new bronze lamp |
| 33 | iron | a new golf club . . . or a whole set |
| 34 | food | take a cooking class together |
| 35 | coral | a coral bead necklace |
| 36 | antiques | go to a flea market together to find treasures |
| 37 | books | choose an audiobook to listen to together in the car |
| 38 | luck | give a shamrock pendant or other lucky charm |
| 39 | laughter | see an improv show |
| 40 | ruby | share an anniversary toast with ruby red wineglasses |
| 41 | office | a globe with a heart sticker where you got married |
| 42 | clocks | a goofy clock for the man cave |
| 43 | entertainment | see a show at a venue you've never been to before |
| 44 | electronics | the coolest new phone there is |
| 45 | sapphire | visit a blues club or go to an R&B concert |

| 46 | games | go to a sporting event |
| 47 | garden/plants | plant a tree together |
| 48 | home improvement | get that repair you've been putting off |
| 49 | copper | new cookware |
| 50 | gold | a bouquet of golden roses, sunflowers, or daffodils |
| 51 | photos/cameras | get a professional photo portrait taken of you both |
| 52 | bath/spa | spend an afternoon at a day spa |
| 53 | plastic | a gift card to his or her favorite store |
| 54 | glass | a special ornament for the Christmas tree |
| 55 | emerald | anything to wear in that vivid hue |
| 56 | day | go on a lunch date |
| 57 | night | a special night on the town |
| 58 | faith and hope | an uplifting book or collection of inspirational music |
| 59 | charity | donate and get your names on a brick or plaque |
| 60 | diamond | stay at a hotel or B&B with "diamond" in the name |

# Soul Mates Celebrate: Halloween

Even grown-ups like to dress up sometimes. Here are some costume ideas that could make you the coolest couple at the party (like you weren't already).

- Wildlife Photographer and Lion: All the photographer needs is a utility vest, a safari hat, and, of course, a camera.
- Night and Day: One person wears black clothing decorated all over with silver stars; the other wears an all-yellow outfit and sunglasses.
- Firefigher and Fire: For a "fire" costume, wear all orange clothing accented with flame decals, which are sold to decorate cars and motorcycles.
- Or, Firefighter and Dalmatian
- Princess and Frog
- Bonnie and Clyde
- Fisherman and Mermaid
- Sheriff and Saloon Lady (or Outlaw)
- Magician and Rabbit

- Sherlock Holmes and John Watson
- Astronaut and Alien
- Frida Kahlo and Diego Rivera
- Disco Dancers
- Antony and Cleopatra
- Football or Basketball Player and Referee
- Angel and Devil
- Ringmaster and Clown
- Pharaoh and Egyptian Queen
- Pirate and Parrot
- Race Car Driver and Mechanic
- Elf and Reindeer, if you're already looking forward to Christmas!

# Soul Mates in History

## Pierre and Marie Curie

In 1891, Polish universities didn't admit women. "Fine," said Maria Sklodowska, and she went to Paris to study. Marie, as they called her there, spent a lot of time in the laboratory. The director, Pierre Curie, spent a lot of time studying her.

Marie agreed with his hypothesis that they should be married. Together, they enjoyed traveling, long bicycle rides, and discovering things like spontaneous radioactivity, which won them the Nobel Prize. Whether they're making scientific breakthroughs, parenting, or repainting the hallway, great couples know how to work together.

# Some Little Ways to Say "I Love You"

- Hold hands for no reason at all.
- Text in the middle of the day just to say hi.
- Tell him, "You look amazing."
- Buy "her" snack at the store.
- Write a love note in chalk on the driveway.
- Send her a card in the mail.
- Buy a first place blue ribbon and put it where he'll find it. Write in the category, such as "Best Husband."

# Soul Mates Celebrate: Birthdays
(You might want to use one of these ideas for Valentine's Day, too.)

- Think bubbly: bubble bath and champagne.
- Make a list of reasons you love him as long as the number of years he's lived.
- Give a serious present with a sentimental card and a ridiculous present with a funny card.
- Conspire with his boss to get him a surprise day off, and spend the day having fun.
- Hide love notes where she'll be sure to find them: in the kitchen, the car, coat pockets, the bathroom, by the computer, and so on.
- Get the day off to a good start by going out to breakfast.

- Sneak a birthday candle in his muffin.
- Throw her a surprise party . . . but only if you're sure she will love the attention!
- Give him a watch or piece of jewelry inscribed with a sweet message and the date.

"Tell me what it was I did to deserve you and I'll do it again, a million times over."

# Challenge

# Beach Glass

When a couple first gets together,
they have no way to know
all that will come their way.
Life changes. People change.
They have to make sure
not to drift apart
but to stay side by side,
like two bright pieces
of glass on a beach . . .
experience shapes them
into smooth, glowing stones,
not what they used to be,

**but even more beautiful.**

STACEY DONOVAN

> We will have our **rose years** and our dandelion times. We will know what tears are, and laughter, too.

But through it all, our **love will bloom.**
And I will always be in love with you. "

CHERYL HAWKINSON

# How to Chase Away Your Partner's Blues

Everybody gets down sometimes, and you're there to help pick each other back up. Here are some ways to do that . . .

- If she's stressed, give her a shoulder rub . . . or a foot rub.
- Encourage him to go to bed on time and get a good night's sleep.
- Play her favorite song in the car.
- Hide a silly card or note where he'll find it later.
- Watch a funny movie or TV show with her.
- Bring him a donut from a donut shop for breakfast.
- Hug her and squeeze tight.

"The clouds make the sunrise

even more beautiful."

# Nine Rules for Fighting Right

1. Are you sure this is even worth fighting about?

2. Seriously, are you really sure? Will you even care a year from now? A month from now? Maybe you should just take a time-out and do something else. You might realize before long that it's not a big deal.

3. No yelling. This is hard if you grew up in a house where people yelled a lot. But it gets easier with practice, like anything else.

4. Absolutely no name-calling.

5. Stay on topic—no bringing up other things you don't like.

**6 Listen to what the other person is saying. There are two sides to just about everything.**

7 Suggest compromises.

8 If you've been harsh or unfair, say you're sorry.

9 Tell your partner you love him or her.

# Ten Ways to Make Up

1. do a load of laundry

2. bring home chocolate

3. order out for pizza

4. puppy eyes

5. write a letter about how much you love her and why

6. tell him what you're going to do to make sure you don't have that argument again

7. give her a foot rub

8. . . . you know

9. say, "I'm sorry"

10. say, "I love you"

# "In this home . . .

We do second chances.
We do grace.
We do real.
We do mistakes.
We do I'm sorrys.
We do loud really well.
We do hugs.
We do family.
We do love."

SARAH MAGILL

# Soul Mates in History

## Robert and Elizabeth Barrett Browning

Robert and Elizabeth were two of the most prominent poets of the Victorian era. How was their love a challenge? Let us count the ways.

1. Robert fell in love with Elizabeth's poetry and then her, but because she was six years older than he and an invalid, it took time to convince her of his affections.

2. When they eloped, Elizabeth's father promptly disinherited her, and her brothers cut off contact as well because they thought Robert lacked class.

3. Elizabeth suffered four miscarriages before finally having a son at the age of 43.

Despite their early challenges and Elizabeth's ongoing health problems, the couple inspired each other to write masterful poetry and enjoyed a romantic and harmonious marriage. Their love letters to each other and the life they shared are a testament to how love can overcome many obstacles.

**hand-holder**

**child wrangler**

**laundry doer**

**errand runner**

**future planner**

**problem solver**

They did a lot of different jobs.
Some of them were fun. Some of them weren't.

**But their life together was worth it.**

"Love me when I least deserve it,

because that's when I really need it."

SWEDISH PROVERB

If you can't ignore it, face it.
If you can't replace it, repair it.
If you can't fix the whole thing, fix a little bit.
If you can't avoid it, get through it
with chocolate, funny movies, hugs, whatever it takes.
If Plan A is a disaster, and Plan B
isn't looking too good either,
just move on to C and beyond.
Hold hands. Stand tall. Say,

> "Trouble, we are not afraid of you.
> Our love is deeper than you
> and it's stronger than you
> and it'll still be here
> long after you're gone."

STACEY DONOVAN

> Love doesn't mind
> if you make lousy coffee.
> Love will still kiss you
> when you have the flu.
> Love moves the driver's seat
> back when you need it,
> reminds you to wear sunblock,
> cares if you do . . .
> Love may not have time
> for intimate dinners—
> and sometimes prefers
> a night of TV . . .
> But love will stand by you,
> defend you, remind you . . .
> *You're never alone in this world.*
> *You have me.*

JENNIFER FUJITA

# Renewal

# Ten Things That Long-Married Couples Know How to Do

1 order for each other at restaurants

2 finish each other's sentences

3 *start* each other's sentences

4 get out of going to parties their partners won't want to go to

5 wear coordinating outfits—without even trying

6 find the humor in a bad day

**7** find the humor in a bad *month*

**8** deal with each other's weird families (and all families are weird in their own way)

**9** have as much fun on a Friday night trip to the grocery store as most couples do on a fancy date

**10** remember all the good things the other person has done, while somehow forgetting all the not-so-good things (not-so-good things? we don't remember any.)

We'll always be eighteen
**for each other.**

# Romantic Ways to Stay Healthy

Let's face it—you want to be around for each other for a long time. Here are a few ways to make it fun.

- If you're going out to dinner, choose a place that you can walk to, if at all possible. You'll get a little exercise before and after the meal, and you'll spend some extra time together.

- As kids, some of us got a lollipop after a checkup. For grown-ups, medical appointments aren't very much fun, so we could use some rewards, too. Give her a bouquet of flowers the day she gets a mammogram, or treat him to a little gift when he goes to the dentist.

- Get a stationary bike, treadmill, or rebounder trampoline and take turns using it while you watch TV together.

- Keep all the makings for a main-dish salad ready in the fridge—washed greens, chopped vegetables, roasted diced chicken, and whatever else you like. Then when you come home after a hard day, you can hit your own "salad bar" instead of the drive-through.

- Take dance lessons together. You might even be able to find some for free online. You'll get in better shape as you learn some new moves.

- Buy a bicycle built for two and use it. You will look adorable.

- Did you know that married people live longer, healthier lives than single ones? Just being together is good for you.

"The mixtape of our marriage is full of
slow jams and soul tunes,
gospel choruses and dance tracks,
old-school R&B and jazz ballads—
love songs every one.

The mixtape of our marriage is full of
the call-and-response
of true partnership,
the holy harmony
of predestined soul mates,
and the righteous rhythm
of made-for-each-other lovers.

The mixtape of our marriage is
the sweet soundtrack to this
good, good life we've got together,
and it's going to play
on and on and on."

SARAH MAGILL

# How to Write a Love Note

Want to turn a regular day into a special occasion, and give him something he'll hold onto forever? Here's how.

### Mention why you're writing.
It might be an occasion like Valentine's Day, but *I just felt like telling you* . . . is also a good reason.

### Affirm him.
What are his best qualities? What has he done lately that you're grateful for?

### See the future.
What are you looking forward to together? Seeing him tonight? Still loving him when he's sixty-four?

### Finish strong.
How about: *All my love, Forever yours, Tenderly, XOXOXO, Your loving partner* . . . just to name a few.

KEELY CHACE

# Follow Your Passions

Whether or not you share them, hobbies can offer great opportunities to go to new places and try new things. Here are some ideas for weekend trips or full-fledged vacations based on popular pastimes.

### Reading
Go to the National Book Festival in Washington, D.C., sponsored by the Library of Congress. Many states and cities have smaller book festivals, too.

### Movies
Get passes for a film festival near you.

### Cats
Yes, they have conventions for cat lovers. Why not check one out?

### Dogs
Attend the Westminster Kennel Club Dog Show for a once-in-a-lifetime experience.

### Fishing
Rapid City, South Dakota, is famous for trout fishing, and it's a great home base for exploring the Black Hills.

### Gardening
Visit the Montreal Botanical Garden, which displays more plants than any other garden in North America.

### Hunting
Spend a weekend at a hunting lodge. Some of them offer enough luxury to make even a non-hunter happy to be there.

### Hiking
Hike part of the Appalachian Trail . . . even if it's just a day hike.

## Golf
Home to Myrtle Beach, Hilton Head, and Kiawah Island, South Carolina is a great destination for a golfing vacation.

## Genealogy
Visit a town where one of your ancestors lived, and imagine what life must have been like back then.

## Home Brewing
Attend a home brewers' conference and explore the town where it's held.

## Football
Visit the Pro Football Hall of Fame in Canton, Ohio.

## Home Decorating
Enjoy a tour of homes in your own town or someplace new.

## Camping
Camp at a designated "Dark Sky Park" and see more stars than you've ever seen before.

## Auto Racing
Make a stock car race a highlight of a weekend getaway.

## Bird Watching
Visit a refuge during migratory season.

## Running
Run a race in a town you've never visited before.

## Photography
Drive to a historical town or a ghost town and get a lot of great shots.

## Woodworking
Take a woodworking class at Arrowmont School of Arts and Crafts in Gatlinburg, Tennessee, as part of a vacation to the Great Smoky Mountains.

# Little Habits You Can Change to Make a Big Difference

You never want to take the person you love for granted. Here are a few ways to let your partner know you love and respect him or her just as much as ever.

- Kiss goodbye and hello.
- When you want to talk to him, go to him rather than hollering from another room.
- Don't walk so fast that she can't keep up with you.
- Call when you're going to be late.

- Compliment him or brag about him to other people.
- Say "please" and "thank you."
- Look at her when she's talking to you.
- That bad habit she keeps nagging you about? Change it.
- That bad habit you keep nagging her about? Let it go.

"Someday, when we have been
together for a very long time,
we'll turn out the lights
and slow-dance on the porch
in our bathrobes.
I'll write you love notes
in large print
and tape them to the fridge.
You'll finish my stories,
and I'll borrow your glasses.
We'll wonder where the time went.
And each night,
we'll roll to the middle
of our old bed,
into one another's arms,
where we'll kiss and touch
and dream the secret dreams
that only old lovers know."

LINDA STATEN

"And each night,
we'll roll to the middle
of our old bed . . ."

# What's Your Secret?

**We asked some longtime couples, "What's your secret to having a successful relationship?"**

"I think one secret to having a successful relationship is to really care about what makes the other person happy. My wife is into photography, so I encourage her to pursue it. I try to be her biggest cheerleader! It is my way of showing her that I care about her happiness."

"Our relationship works because we are at the age where we don't want to change each other. We ignore the flaws and celebrate the things we love. We don't nag each other, and ironically, because we want to make each other happy, we change. Not because it was demanded, but because we want to be the best partner we can be."

"Space. Give it to him. And make sure to carve out your own. We're stronger together when we have time to be ourselves."

"My husband and I do what works for our relationship and don't get hung up on gender roles. Because he teaches school and I work an office job with longer hours, it makes sense for him to do more cooking for our family and caregiving for our kids than I do."

"Like any couple, we get on each other's nerves sometimes. But I've learned that our relationship, like most long-term things in life, is cyclical. Like a career, or being a mom, or any other big thing, I know now that a bad day doesn't automatically spell trouble . . . I know that it all comes back around and that within days, I'll forget whatever it was that made me mad and think he's perfect again soon."

"Patience, humor, and constant foundation repair. Fill in those cracks before they can even appear."

"Less talking, more touching. At least in my love relationship, physical affection (not necessarily sex) is almost always more effective than words at soothing hurt feelings, expressing love, and making us feel close."

"Giving the benefit of the doubt really helps. People aren't perfect, so it helps to assume that the person you love doesn't want to hurt you, even if they do sometimes."

"We both think we're the lucky one."

## I keep a mental scrapbook of our life together—

a collection of memories and
the many things I love about you.
There are clippings from birthdays and holidays . . .
ticket stubs from the laughable, tearful,
and romantic moments we've shared . . .
vivid snapshots of you
as you smile at me across the room
or laugh at one of our shared jokes.
But I also keep
a delicate little piece of your voice tucked away
just like it sounds when whispering softly in the night . . .
and some of the feeling I have
when you curl up to me on a cold winter's morning—
the warmth of your skin next to mine.
I have a sample of your cologne . . .
and even a wing from the butterflies
you sent aflutter in my stomach
when we first met.

I turn to these mental pages
during a busy day when we're apart
or when I just want to indulge the love I feel for you.
But I know there are so many more moments to add,
so many memories to make.

{ **I will treasure each one of them just as I treasure you— always.** }

What keeps you and your
soul mate living in love?
We'd love to hear from you.

Please send your comments to:
Hallmark Book Feedback
P.O. Box 419034
Mail Drop 100
Kansas City, MO 64141

Or e-mail us at:
booknotes@hallmark.com